More Dartmoor Letterboxes

by

ANNE SWINSCOW

KIRKFORD PUBLICATIONS

First published December 1986
by Kirkford Publications
Cross Farm, Diptford, Totnes, Devon
Reprinted 1995

My first book on Dartmoor Letterboxes was dedicated to the "Nut-cases" who spend their spare time hunting for these boxes on Dartmoor. This too is dedicated to them, but especially to all those "Nut-cases" who have, knowingly, or unknowingly, provided me with material – Thank-you very much, Dartmoor would not be the same without you....

....as Dame Margaret Rutherford put it:- "...there is more latitude in eccentrics. They are always honest, and have their own quality of madness. In the final assessment, I think they will be the saints."

Printed and bound in Great Britain by
BPC Wheatons Ltd, Exeter

ISBN 0 9509114 1 0

CONTENTS

ILLUSTRATIONS

Photo on page 19 by Jean leaman, pages 53 and 59 by D. Wyn Hughes, page 61 by Brenda Williams, pages 49, 67 and 75 by Anne Swinscow, all other photos by Daro Montag.

INTRODUCTION

If you are already a letterbox hunter, or if you have read "Dartmoor Letterboxes", please excuse the following explanations, or if you like – turn over the page and miss this bit out.

So you decided to read on, well in that case you probably have no idea what this book is all about, and the nearest you have ever come to a Dartmoor Letterbox is the red G.P.O. letterbox at Postbridge.

The idea of Letterboxes on Dartmoor originated in 1854 when a Dartmoor guide, named James Perrott placed a bottle in a bank at Cranmere Pool as a receptacle for the cards of the intrepid walkers that he had escorted there. This idea was described by one Victorian authority as "a snare for Tourists", but if one was taking a guided walk on the moor it was useful to have a goal, and, having reached that goal, a method of recording the fact. At that time there was of course no Military ring road, so the walk to Cranmere was sufficiently difficult to be worth recording. Leaving ones calling card was the "Kilroy was here" of the times.

By 1888 a tin box had replaced the bottle, and in 1905 a visitors book was provided and gradually one's signature in the book took over from the calling cards. Later a rubber stamp and ink pad were added and it became fashionable to leave a post card addressed to oneself or a friend in the box, this would be stamped by the next caller to the box and posted on (via a more conventional letterbox) from his home town. In 1937 the site was taken over by the Western Morning News, and a granite box erected to replace the cairn. This box, built like a miniature stone hut, still stands, it is in fact the only Dartmoor Letterbox that in any way resembles its G.P.O. counterpart, and one of the only two that have any permanent structure at all – the other being at Duck's Pool.

1

Duck's Pool letterbox dates from 1938. The box was set up by a group of walkers known as Dobson's Moormen, in memory of William Crossing the Dartmoor writer and gazetteer. In addition to being a memorial to a great Dartmoor figure, it was intended to be a focal point for walks on the South Moor, in the same way as Cranmere Pool was for the North Moor, though by this time the Military road had been built and to get to Cranmere no longer posed so much of a challenge. Both boxes were strategically placed, one at the centre of the North Moor and one at the centre of the South Moor, and for some years these two were the only Letterboxes on Dartmoor. (With the doubtful exception of the secret and undiscovered Belstone Box.)

By 1976 there were fifteen known boxes on the moor, and these were described in an illustrated chart, designed to provide interesting walks on the moor. This chart proved so popular that people started putting out other boxes to provide other sites to visit, and from then on letterboxes suffered a population explosion. Boxes were sited here, there and everywhere, sometimes not too wisely, so after much debate a code of conduct was thought up. This is designed to protect the antiquities of the moor and to insure that letterboxers and letterboxes cause the minimum of upset to the landowners, commoners and other moor users.

The code is as follows:-
Boxes should not be sited,
1. In any kind of Antiquity. In or near Stone-rows or Circles, Cists or Cairns. Or in any kind of Buildings, Walls or Ruins, Peatcutters or Tinners Huts, etc.
2. In any potentially dangerous situation where injuries could be caused.
3. As a fixture. Cement or any other building material not to be used.
Boxhunters should follow the country code.

So though there may be up to 1,000 boxes out at a time, only Cranmere Pool and Duck's Pool will be visible to the casual observer.

The modern letterbox is usually contained in an old ammunition tin, or any other waterproof container, and before anyone has a fit at the thought of 1,000 or so of these littering up Dartmoor, I would suggest they go out and have a look for themselves. If you don't know where to look I would defy you to find any. But you do not need to be equipped with your garden spade before you join the hunt, though well concealed, these boxes are not three feet underground. You are more likely to come across a box if you look between a crack in the rocks, in a natural niche in a peat bank or, masked by heather, under a boulder. Find one box, and in the visitors book you may well find clues to another. If you want to go letterboxing in comfort, try the Plume of Feathers at Princetown, The Kings Arms at Okehampton, The Rock Inn at Haytor Vale or the Museum of Dartmoor Life at Okehampton, at these places of course you don't have to search for the visitors book and stamp, just ask for it.

I must warn anyone new to letterboxing that each box ought to carry a government health warning .... letterboxing is addictive! However, if you get hooked you will find that you have an absorbing hobby that will take you all over Dartmoor to places you never knew existed, you will take a great deal of healthy exercise and you will make a lot of new friends, but if you are not careful it will take over your life, so don't forget, IT'S ONLY A GAME.

Chapter 1

Why do people go letterboxing? Well why do we take up any leisure pursuit? If you think that hunting for little boxes in the wilds of Dartmoor sounds daft, then consider a few other spare-time occupations. Take golf for an example. Golfers are usually perfectly rational, sensible people whose main source of enjoyment is toting a heavy bag of angled rods across country in all weathers in order to have the privilege of hitting a small white ball along in front of them. Put like that does it sound a rational occupation?

One definition of cricket is ... "casting a ball at three straight sticks, and defending the same with a fourth", and if you start talking about "square legs" and "silly mid-offs" to a foreigner you could well bring forth some odd looks. Yet cricket is a highly respectable game, taught in schools alongside such commonplace subjects as English and Mathematics, (though as yet there is no C.S.E. certificate for Cricket!).

The sport of board-sailing looks either great fun, or masochistic, depending which way you happen to see it. But standing on a small fin, in mid ocean with your arms being pulled out of their sockets and with the imminent and frequent prospect of being dunked into remarkably cold water, is the regular weekend pursuit of many. One could reason that most leisure activities are a bit odd, and letterboxing is no odder than most.

Our ancestors' days were filled with the ever pressing task of finding enough to eat, but as man developed into farming groups and work became more organised, he had time to think of other things, and the leisure industry was invented. Probably one of the earliest records of this would be the cave

Duck's Pool box … a focal point for walks on the South Moor….

paintings and rock carvings of Neolithic time. Mundane, useful objects were decorated, some with religious significance, but many just for the joy of decoration. Bones were carved with ornate patterns, and later pottery was decorated and beautiful things were made of bronze and other metals.

The first sports to develop were based on the age-old themes of war and hunting. The best spear throwers, archers and runners won the battles. They also won the Olympic Games. The fastest horses could win races as well as wars. A wild boar was a welcome addition to a dull winter diet in Norman times, but the chase could also be a social event. A later generation no longer hunted for food, the "trophy of the chase" became the object of the exercise, and sporting (or unsporting) remains were displayed in many a house. Study and billiard room walls were hung with aloof antelope heads, snarling lions and wide antlered moose. While even the nursery rug might be a tiger or polar-bear, relegated from the drawing room because the moth had got at it! A walk through the Torquay Antique shops reveals the interests of a generation. Indian brasses, elephant foot umbrella stands and rhinoceros horn walking sticks, all lovingly collected by the British abroad.

At home the British were collecting too. Houses contained boxes of neatly displayed butterflies, books of pressed flowers etc. Small boys were encouraged to make collections of birds'-eggs, "Edwardian Ladies" collected and painted wild flowers. When Napoleon called the British a "Nation of Shopkeepers" he might have been more accurate had he referred to us as a nation of collectors. Cigarette card collecting was a long lasting phenomenon that was only killed by war-time austerity, but since the war collecting has become almost a mania.

Broadly speaking collecting can be sub-divided under two headings: 1. Items purchased, and 2. Items found. Of course many of the items purchased involve a hunt, especially if one collects anything of an antique or bygone type. Sales and Flea-markets advertise items as "collectables", which covers any items from silver spoons to old post-cards or rusted biscuit tins from another era, but even if acquired for 5p from a junk

Most regular letterboxers have what is known as a "personal stamp".

stall this sort of collection must still be "bought".

The other kind of collection – items found – can cover two types of objects. Those that are made by nature and those that are made by man. One of my hobbies is fossil hunting, and to me there is a great thrill in finding the remains of a creature that may have lived 50,000,000 years ago, but to other people my collection may look just a lot of old stones. Talking of stones, many people collect mineral samples (in fact I have about 50 myself), but there are plenty of other types of "natural" collections.

There are not so many different "man-made" collections that can be had for free. Stamp collections can start with what comes through the letterbox, but you will soon find yourself buying to boost your collection, and autograph hunting is limited, so perhaps that accounts for the phenomenal way that Letterboxing has caught on. It combines the fact that almost everyone loves collecting, with the added excitement of a treasure hunt and the excuse to go out and enjoy the beauties of Dartmoor. What more could anyone want?

Chapter 2

THE MAD HATTERS

100 CLUB

1986

Letterboxing is a great leveller. In what other sport, pastime or hobby could you find a retired Naval Commander struggling to keep ahead of a Brownie Pack? Or a Company Director doing "swaps" with a ten-year old schoolboy? One can start at any age (babies have been known to be carried in slings on their first boxing excursions), and continue for as long as your legs will carry you. While many boxes are of course in the middle of the moor, a great number are to be found within half a kilometre of the road.

Finance too does not come into it. Naturally if you have a car and can afford the petrol for regular outings, then you may (like the lager in the advertisement) get to the parts that others can't reach. But plenty of letterboxers go out to the moor by bicycle, bus or Shanks' Pony. Money may buy you better boots, the latest in waterproof outfits and duck-down filled parkas, but it will *not* find you letterboxes. All you need for this is strong footwear, sensible clothing and a good map and compass – plus of course a little inside information.

This is the most difficult part, how does one start? The answer is – modestly. Don't expect to rush out and find 800 letterboxes all in one go. Find the old established boxes that are on the survey map, and visit the "Pub" boxes if you wish. Looking carefully through the visitors book at any of these will probably give you the clues to other boxes, and so it goes on, one thing will lead to another. If progress seems slow to start with, remember that it is just as slow to the old hands. Every area of the moor will have boxes that are new to you, but when you have been at it for years and collected all that are available you will have to make a long trip for *one* new stamp each time one comes out. Most letterboxers are willing to help those who are new to the hobby, and you are almost certain to meet other boxers out on the moor who will advise you of boxes in the area. However, if someone seems to be secretive about the whereabouts of a box or boxes, please don't think letterboxers are a nasty lot, boxes can be vandalised and they are probably just being careful.

When you have collected 100 boxes you are entitled to join the "100 Club". This is a club that does not exist, there is no committee, no premises and no benefits. The only rule for membership is that you must have visited 100 different letterboxes. NOT just collected 100 different stamps. When you reach this goal you are entitled to wear the 100 Club badge, a white cloth badge with the words "Dartmoor Letterboxes 100 Club".

Letterboxers are an honest lot, and if you say you have been to 100 boxes your word is taken, should you cheat just to get a badge you would be hurting no one but yourself. Other letterboxers have a pretty good idea how often your name has appeared in the visitors books around the moor, and would be pretty scornful if a newcomer was seen to be wearing a 100 club badge, or a summer holiday boxhunter claimed to have visited 1,000 boxes.

For those who have proved they are serious letterboxers there is a book of clues available. At the time of writing this is brought out twice a year, but such is the changing population of boxes, that it is always out of date before it is in print, so there is no surefire way of knowing where every box is on the moor at any given time. For real up to date information boxers ring each other up, produce news-sheets, or send out postcards showing new stamps. Information on new boxes is traded, and when only a cryptic clue is given as to the whereabouts of a new box, there is keen competition as to who can crack it first.

Cryptic clues take some thinking out, and several boxes have sat on the moor unvisited while boxers struggle to come up with the correct answer. Clues such as "Short Red Pencil", "Swallow Quickly", "Where Time Stands Still" and "Christian Farm Holiday" may take months to unravel. Anagrams are usually simpler to solve, one can usually start by extracting the letters for TOR, LAKE, ROCK, or some other descriptive word, and then work on the remaining letters. For example – PRESS USSR CROLL. If one takes the word "CROSS" out of that one is left with PREUSSRLL, and a look at the map or Crossing's Guide will show you that the other word can only be "SPURRELLS", so one arrives at Spurrells Cross. One just needs a little Dartmoor knowledge and a lot of dedication.

Chapter 3

Most regular letterboxers have what is known as a "personal stamp". These are used to sign in the letterbox visitors books, and they vary from simple designs cut at home out of rubbers, to elaborate pictures on professionally produced stamps. Toy shops and stationers now stock small pictorial designs on stamps, these are cheap to buy, and usually portray fictitious characters such as Snoopy, Winnie the Pooh or the Mister Men, or animals, teddy bears or dolls. These stamps reproduce very well, and a lot of children have them as their personal stamp. Adult personal stamps very often are a pun on the name of the owner, or the place where they live, or have some reference to one of the features of Dartmoor.

It is surprising how often BOGS feature in the names walkers give themselves. There are the "Okehampton Boghoppers", "The Bog Sinker and Stinker", "Slab the Boghopper" and "The St Thomas More's Bogtrotters"; obviously they have walked the Moor in all its moods! Other Dartmoor feature names include "Duck's Pool Dabblers", "Dartmoor Ramblers", "The Clitter Climbers", "Dartmoor Granite Grinders", "The Moorlovers" and "The Dartmoor Drifter".

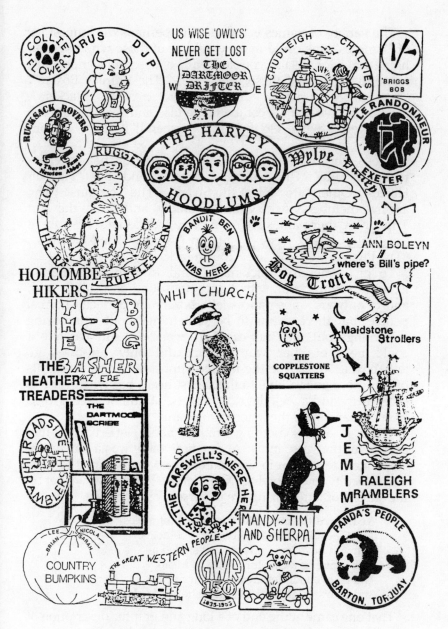

... they vary from simple designs to elaborate pictures.

The variety of names is infinite, but perhaps the longest list of "handles" one could make would be of those who use their home town or village coupled with a descriptive noun. To name just a few of these, there are:- "The Brimley Boxers", "Topsham Tourists", "The Exeter Heather Hackers", "Exmouth Five", "Holecombe Hopefuls" and the "Clearbrook Clamberers", while Godfrey (my husband) is the "Diptford Letterbox Hound".

Those who use their family name as part of their letterbox name include "The Hiking Hoopers" and the "Hawker Hikers". Others are "Nigel the Swan", "The Torquins" (who are five members of the Quintrell family) and "Mike the Turf Tripper". Other names are even more individual – how about the "Wild Goose Chasers", "Stamp Tramp", "The Mudlarks", "The Plym-Souls" and the "Cousin Jacks".

To give oneself a nick-name, and to sign oneself in a letterbox visitors book with it does not sound particularly odd, and to outward appearances letterboxers are perfectly normal people, but there seems to be something about letterboxing that brings out the "nut-case" in everyone. Alternatively it could be the other way round, and only nut-cases go letterboxing, or maybe the rarified atmosphere on the heights of Dartmoor goes a little to the sanest head, but whatever it is eccentricity and a well developed sense of humour seem to go hand in hand with the letterboxing game.

There is also something strange about letterboxing that brings out the verse in us. At one time there was a box where everyone had to sign in with a poem, no one seemed to have any difficulty in complying. Many of the letters that we get on the subject of letterboxing are in verse. For example:-

> We hunted the moor like a keen pair of moles
> But still couldn't find the box at Woolholes.
> So if you have laughed – or just smiled at this read
> Please give us a clue for Leamans Mead.
> And be even kinder, aware of our needs
> And throw in another to find Bishops Meads.

That one came at the end of a long and graphic description of a fruitless hunt for the three boxes mentioned.

The variety of names is infinite....

Another one from a family applying for their 100 club badges goes as follows:-

Thro' rain or mist or blistering heat,
With soggy socks and tired feet;
We've tramped the moor for many a mile
Sometimes it didn't make us smile!

Our quest? Those boxes – hidden well,
But they were there so we'd heard tell.
In holes on Tors or in peat hags,
Many in Tesco's carrier bags!
Within each box a different stamp,
Some of them were *very* damp!

Kind friends supplied us with more clues,
And every month sent us the news –
Of boxes taken in or new
When first we had but very few.

But now, dear sir, we have enough
To claim a badge and other stuff;
One hundred stamps are in our book
So next weekend we start to look
For other boxes to be had –
We sometimes think we must be mad!

But after all is said and done
It really is tremendous fun.
We've learned a lot about the moor
And country folk who've gone before,
Their lives and ways and legends too –
"We're Off!" for hundred number two.

I think the writer of that poem (the mother of two teenagers) has got it right. One letterboxer has a rational reason for the poetic side of boxing, in one of her letters to Godfrey she ends with a P.S.:- "We are trying to keep up the poetic theme as we travel from box to box. It's good fun – and it keeps the old 'grey matter' exercised, as well as the legs! It's surprising how habitual it can become when one gets stuck into the spirit of the game!" What could be better than fun combined with healthy exercise for the mind and body – it beats jogging any day!

Chapter 4

Eccentricity combined with a sense of fun have produced some wonderful ideas in letterboxers. Who but a letterboxer would have thought of issuing passports to the North Moor? Who but a letterboxer would have suggested "street lights" on the Military ring road? crazy paving in the peat-passes? or opening a beer garden at the military post "O.P.17"? The ideas seem endless, and letters and questionnaires go back and forth between such characters as "Signor S.P. Ghetti", proprietor of the "O.P. 15 Pizzaria", and his friends.

For anyone reading this who may have conservationist leanings I would hasten to explain that all these things are entirely fictitious and exist only on paper. (Though some are also on photographic paper, as the instigators of these fun fantasies have gone to the trouble of taking props out to the Moor, including cafe umbrellas, sauce bottles etc. and photographing them *in situ*.)

The first of these little oddities was probably the North Dartmoor Passport. It started after there had been a spot of bother with boxes being vandalized and the rubber stamps taken. As everyone knows most of the ills that befall one on the Moor are caused by Pixies, so a passport was issued to protect selected letterboxers, and with each passport a certificate was issued.

Each passport-holder was given a personal code number, all VERY serious. At the end of the certificate came a restriction:- "Not transferable. This passport is not valid to the Foreign Lands south of the B3212 and B3357 roads" and all holders of passports had to sign a declaration that they were of sound mind.

One wonders!

The next bit of fun and games was the "Street lights for the Ring road" campaign. There had been talk of digging up the ring road and letting the area revert to open moor, a fine thought for conservationists, but a sad thought for the many who use the road to give them access to walks on the North Moor. In the end it was decided to let the road suffer "benign neglect", in other words not to maintain it with a tarmac surface, but to let it gradually revert to a pot-holed track, a compromise that probably pleased most people. But, in the meantime, a "save the ring road campaign" had been going on, and among other ideas came the suggestion of street lamps. One thing led to another and eventually a fictitious organisation known as:- (and I quote) "...the Light All Moorland Paths Society, or LAMPS...the pilot group will be known as the Dartmoor Inaugural Members of LAMPS, or DIM LAMPS."

A questionnaire and application form for those wanting to join DIM LAMPS was sent out. Among the questions asked was, "Are you prepared to do voluntary work on any DIM LAMP project? If yes, do you own (1) a JCB, (2) a road drill, (3) a tea urn, please give details of any other expertise or equipment you could make available" the only thing we could offer in reply was "a pack of hounds for feasibility studies of suitable lamp post sites."

Members of DIM LAMPS were invited to attend an Inaugural Meeting at 8 a.m. on Tuesday 25th December. I don't know how many people replied to this invitation, but our reply stated that we would be unable to attend because we were attending a small party at..."sub-station 662 763 on December 24th at 11.45 p.m. We will be entertaining Mr. S. Clause and his assistant Ray N. Dere, and they have kindly

The "Beer Garden" at O.P. 17.

promised to switch on the fairy lights in Two Brothers Adit, Hen Roost Mine and Hooten Wheals, thus beautifying three of the darker spots of Dartmoor.... It was hoped that the stringing of fairy lights between the trees in Wistman's Wood would be completed by this date, but as they will not be ready by the 24th we are arranging for the very Rev. Father Tyme to switch these on, on December 31st at 11.59 p.m."

If you are not a letterboxer, or do not have a knowledge of Dartmoor, the talk of streetlit ring roads and illuminated adits (or mine shafts) probably sounds a lot of nonsense. In fact, like Lewis Carrol's Jabberwock – nonsense it is. But as Alice found that Jabberwocky made sense to her after an explanation, I will attempt to make sense of what I have written. First look at an ordnance survey map of Dartmoor. The ring road is the track marked with a dotted line, that runs out into the North Moor from the Army camp at Okehampton. The name "Ring Road" may bring to mind an urban by-pass, but think again, this track by-passes nothing more than the odd boggy patch, only the fact that it meanders round the bleak landscape in a loop earns it the name of "ring" road. But most ring roads have street lights – and so fantasy takes over.

Fairy lights in adits? Well several letterboxes, commemorating the old tin mines on the moor have been placed in, or near adits. Anyone looking for a letterbox in the dark mouth of an adit would appreciate a torch, so why not fairy lights for the benefit of all letterboxers? Do you know Wistman's Wood? It is a most beautiful, but eerie strip of oak forest, sited up the West Dart from Two Bridges. Of great interest to botanists, it consists of a strip of stunted oaks, several hundred years old, but none much taller than a large shrub. The trees grow out of a tumbled mass of granite and they are hung with mosses and lichens till the whole place looks like an Arthur Rackham illustration, one could imagine anything happening there, and I am sure Old Father Time would feel quite at home. But if you like the Disneyland outlook on life – you would appreciate it even more with fairy lights. (Or, an idea which I hadn't thought of before, with Snow White and the Seven Dwarfs living in the middle.)

Fairy Lights in Wistman's Wood!

If you look again at the Ordnance Survey map, the sub-station 662 763 is actually Snaily House, a ruin that has featured in many a letterbox hunt.

Crazy-paving in the peat passes? Well, why not. (For the benefit of those who may not know what a peat pass is, I will explain that they are cuttings that link bog-free sections of the North Moor. Some, though by no means all are marked on the Ordnance Survey maps and a few, such as Cut Lane and the North West Passage have names. The oldest may originate from Saxon times, but most were cut, or re-cut by Frank Phillpotts around the turn of the century. These cuttings, or passes through the peat have been used by farmers, drovers and the hunts, and they provide safe passage through the bogs for man and beast.)

When letterboxers started using them, it was suggested they might be "wearing them out", hence the suggestion of crazy-paving! Of course this would provide the added bonus of letterboxing without getting your boots muddy.

The "improvements" one might make to the Moor are endless, but one likes to think it is as God made it; and with the exception of Bronze Age hut circles, Iron Age farms, Saxon villages, medieval enclosures, tin workings, copper mines, quarries, clay workings, reservoirs, pylons, farms and roads, so it is!

Chapter 5

Believe it or not, it is perfectly possible to go letterboxing without being mad. The only real necessity is a love of Dartmoor in all its moods, hunting those little boxes is only part of the game. The "Clitter Climbers" expressed this love of the moor, that all of us feel – but few can put on paper, in their poem:- "My Lady Fair"

How I love you Lady Fair.
Haughty, grand, head in air.
Cold, aloof, yet unashamed.
Fenced and mauled but quite untamed.

Tors and hills, hollows and girts,
All layed out on your crumpled skirts.
Mines and cairns and of course the leat.
I lay flowers at your feet.

The men who came in days of yore,
Farmed your land and dug for ore.
Copper, tin, silver and lead,
They cut you deep, oh how you bled.

The scars are there for all to see,
Now they've healed so naturally.
Time and nature have united
To beautify what man has blighted.

Cradled in your mighty arms
Tension evaporates with your charms.
Within your vast and beautiful sphere
Worldly troubles disappear.

Sitting beside a lonely Tor,
Looking below at the valley floor;
Watching the stream meandering by,
Quiets the heart and gladdens the eye.

Many miles I've walked today,
Watched the lambs and birds at play.
Skylark, buzzard, peregrine,
All these wonders I have seen.

From the Hill of Graves to Tavy Cleave,
All your beauty I must leave.
For now, alas, it's time to go –
Dartmoor how I love you so.

With heavy heart and leaden feet,
I begin my slow retreat.
Watching the sunset as I go
Giving your hair an auburn glow.

Please don't leave me, I couldn't stand
The thought of you in another's hand.
My heart would break with such despair.
Oh, how I love you Lady Fair.

Perhaps some people start hunting for boxes without really noticing their surroundings. Head down, compass in hand, they stride along searching for a … "lone tree with a clump of heather on a rock twenty paces on a bearing 250°'", but sooner or later they will lift their heads and take a look about them – then the magic of Dartmoor grabs them. Some people started letterboxing because they loved Dartmoor, other people love Dartmoor because they go letterboxing, either way you are hooked.

People think they are having a nice day out on Dartmoor as they sit, Dad in his deck chair armed with his fags and paperback book (it being too windy for the Sunday paper). Mum putting down her knitting to make the tea on the camping-gaz stove. Grannie dozing behind the windbreak. Teenager with a vacant expression, earphones relaying endless pop music, or, more recently, ghetto blaster ruining the peace, and junior belting his football at the remaining upright of a hut-circle. Well, I am sure they are having a nice day in their own way, and I'm sure it does them good, but are they enjoying Dartmoor? They might be anywhere, their car is an extension of their home, and they will not stray more than 50 yards from it.

Herewith lies the charm of letterboxing. Leave the car-parks, ice-cream vans and kite fliers behind and head for the open moor. One hundred yards from the car-park you will have it to yourself, there may be several hundred other letterboxers about, but there are 365 square miles of moor in front of you, plenty of space for all. If you should be slightly infirm, or encumbered with tiny children, there is no need to despair. You may not be able to reach all the more inaccessible boxes, but there are plenty hidden in enchanting sites within half a mile from the road.

The further you go from the beaten track, the more equipment you will need, and the lonely letterboxer met with in the middle of the North Moor will be wearing walking boots, breeches or strong trousers, gaiters, and an assortment of lumberjack shirts, woolly jerseys and wind-proof jackets according to the weather. On his back will be a vast pack containing a meal, a drink, reserve rations such as chocolate, waterproofs, perhaps a survival blanket and of course, his letterboxing gear. We have even met a lone walker in the centre of the South Moor with an umbrella, one has to be ready for anything.

The letterboxing gear is of course vital. Map and compass are essentials. Maps have a habit of blowing away or getting soggy so a map-case is a good idea. When you start, you may take one copy of each stamp on the back of your map, but soon the map fills up or the stamps get tatty, so you carry a book or some postcards to collect them on. Your own stamp pad and pen are handy, something to press on is a help, and if you have one – you will be carrying your own personal stamp. The difference between a letterboxer and a back-packer is minimal – the letterboxers are the ones without the frying pan tied on their back. Though of course letterboxers can also be back-packers, and back-packers can also be letterboxers. Letterboxers can usually be spotted by the clues in their hands, and their general air of keenness.

The open moor can be compared to the open sea. One of God's great wildernesses, to be enjoyed – but to be treated with respect. A "belt and braces" policy can be applied to both.

Only a fool will set off for a fishing trip in a small outboard dinghy without taking along a pair of oars and a life-jacket for everyone. Only a fool will set off on a walk to the centre of the moor without a few little extras. A hot drink and waterproofs in the winter, and a minimum of a cold drink, a bar of chocolate and a shower proof jacket in summer. (Yes I know the moor is full of streams, but have you thought about that dead sheep that may be lying in the stream above where you are drinking?) Perhaps in really bad weather only a fool (or a letterboxer) would be out on the moor at all, but provided you have proper boots, REALLY waterproof clothes, a compass, a map and some iron rations you are unlikely to come to much harm; though one point that must never be forgotten when you are walking alone is to let someone know where you are walking, and then to walk there and no where else. It is no use telling someone you are walking to Fur Tor, and then jaunting off to Quintin's Man without letting anyone know your change of plan. Accidents happen very rarely, but they can happen. If it is known where to look for you, you will be putting the rescue services to the least possible inconvenience. Why should anyone be expected to give their time and energy – at personal risk – to look for a walker who wasn't where he said he would be?

End of homily!

Chapter 6

So, like all good letterboxers, we are setting off on a boxing expedition. We are wearing all the right gear, and carrying the right equipment. We have been to Cranmere Pool and visited all the right pubs, only one thing is wrong – the pack on our back has no 100 Club badge sewn in the middle.

To some the realisation that they seem to be the only person on the moor without this distinctive badge amounts to a personal challenge. They work at it in a frenzy, every weekend, every light evening and all their holidays they rush about the moor clocking up boxes till at last they triumphantly send their 70p (price at time of writing), and on receiving their badge get busy with needle and thread. Others take a more leisurely attitude, one walker who wrote in claims to be the record holder for the slowest hundred, it took him 20 years, but I bet he enjoyed every minute of it!

On reaching the magical 100, one mother wrote to thank for the badges sent, she concluded her letter thus:- "We certainly won't be hanging up our boots but have decided to limit our trips to every other weekend until we have caught up on our visits to some rather neglected friends." Implying that letterboxing had started to take over – as I warned, it can be addictive. Her two young daughters seem to have got the bug too, having achieved their 100 at the ages of 4 and 6.

Some do not find the first 100 easy though, and we have had some heart-felt letters asking for help. As always with letterbox literature a lot of these seem to come in rhyme, one that came from Bristol went as follows:-

Dear Mrs. Swinscow,
  hear our plea:
Ardent letterboxers we, since in nineteen-seventy-three
We happed on Cranmere Pool.

Since then we've searched each inch of moor –
Heather, bracken, bog and tor, hoping to increase our
  score,
And join the "Hundred Club".

Each year we spend our holiday
Over Moretonhampstead way – also any odd spare day
We play at hunt-the-box.

But Lady Luck's not on our side –
All our efforts she's defied. Though for years and years
  we've tried,
Our score is only six!

So many times we've reached some spot,
Footsore, weary, cold – or hot – looking for a box that's not
Where it ought to be.

Won't you please pass on some clues?
We'll be sad if you refuse. Be assured we won't abuse
Whatever help you give.

Please find enclosed an s.a.e. –
Hoping you'll write back to me. I will gladly send your fee
If you will help us out.

So let us thank you in advance
For the glimmer of a chance our collection to enhance –
And join the "Hundred Club".

Who could refuse a letter like that? The 100 Club, and clue books are not my department, but Godfrey soon put them out of their misery with some clues, and in no time they were claiming their Hundred Club badges.

As with most aspects of letterboxing, and in fact of life in general, things tend to get more organised as time goes on. First it was just a badge for those who attained 100 different boxes. This used to be quite an achievement, when there were say 150 boxes on the moor, to find 100 took a lot of walking. But as more boxes appeared, many of the newer ones tended to be nearer the roads and therefore collecting 100 became less of a feat, and the 100 Club badge appeared on more and more rucksacks. What was to be the next challenge?

So, a 200 and a 500 badge was produced. The design is the same as the 100 badge, but the 200 is on a blue background and the 500 on a gold background. This did not suffice for long, and next a 1,000 badge was produced. To make this special, and quite distinctive from the other badges, this is on a black background and says 1,000 in gold thread, and at the moment is the top achievement badge, though no doubt it will one day be a case of "back to the drawing board" and a 5,000 badge will have to be designed.

These are not, of course, the only badges to be proudly displayed on rucksacks and jackets. Dartmoor has several long-distance walks, such as the annual O.A.T.S. walk from Ivybridge to Okehampton, the North to South walk, the Abbots Way walk and the Ten Post Box walk, badges are available to all who complete these within the official time limits, and as most of them are a severe test of fitness, badges so gained can be worn with pride.

After the 1986 Ten Post Box walk, Phyl Hyett wrote the following poem:-

We met up on a Sunday, the 6th July no less.
At 8.15 we started, all wearing proper dress.
We wore stout boots and sweaters and carried plenty
    more,

With strips of pink Elastoplast in case our feet got sore.
We had to find ten boxes but it was not a race
So we set off walking, the sun upon our face.
South Hessary the first box – only 9 to go.
Sylvia took a photo, so stamping in was slow.
Then Cramber Tor and Older Bridge, Eylesbarrow was a
    drag.
I stopped twice to get my breath. Tony had a fag!
Combshead followed after, then we stopped for lunch.
We sat around on Down Tor, a very merry bunch.
Mervyn spent his lunch break searching for his box
Which previously he'd hidden somewhere in the rocks.
Pete and Cherry helped him, till they too stopped for food;
Finally Merv found it, despite our comments rude!
We staggered on from Down Tor, feeling quite replete,
To Crazywell and Aqueduct, along the Devonport Leat.
A long pull up to Leeden, where I thought I was done,
But Sylv and Rufus cheered me on and soon that box was
    won.
And then we turned to Hart Tor with Black Tor on the
    way,
At last the end came into sight – we'd had a smashing day.

We all "stamped out", well certified and licking sunburnt
    lips
Then straight down into Princetown for steaming fish and
    chips.
Afterwards we gathered in "The Plume" for mugs of beer
Where we sat arranging to go again next year!

Chapter 7

If I made the first 100 sound easy, I would warn you not to be over confident. Kate Smiley and her husband, newly moved to Devon, read "Dartmoor Letterboxes" and decided to have a go. As Kate put it ... "at that time we had vaguely heard about letterboxes, but our image was a rather jumbled one – of some sort of red pillar box cum tupperware." I had, in my book recommended all potential letterboxers to go on the moors prepared with compass, map and some iron rations such as chocolate and apples. I had also given a grid reference – though only a four figure one – to some of the more permanent boxes. Thus armed they confidently set off on their first letterbox hunt, and what followed is directly quoted from the letter Kate sent me afterwards:-

Armed with compass, apples, and lots of chocolate, we strode out briskly along the track to the first grid reference. There, after a lot of searching ...

...we eventually consoled ourselves with some chocolate ...

...and set off for our second grid reference. Better luck on the open moor, we thought.

Oh dear ... again we sat and ate chocolate.

By this time our reserves were beginning to run low – and we still had our third box to "find". – This would be easier because there was a clearly winding stream which helped us get our position just right ... and then we searched ...

...and the mist came down, and still we searched

and the wind howled – but still we poked into every nook and cranny

and the rain poured, – but
intrepidly we kept on.

Until at last we admitted defeat – huddled on the top of a craggy rock …

...and found to our dismay ... that we'd lost the chocolate! So endeth our first day letter-boxing!

A few weeks later I got a much happier letter, also punctuated with Kate's enchanting cartoons. On this expedition they had set off to find seven letterboxes. The first one was found by Dave, Kate's husband, after which they found boxes in turn till the score was three all. Perhaps it was just as well for married bliss that the seventh box was missing, so they were able to go home still on speaking terms, and Kate finished her letter with a poem in the best Dartmoor letterbox tradition.

> We strode out on to Dartmoor,
> We strode at quite a pace,
> To hunt for hidden boxes –
> It soon became a race.
>
> Went up the road some half a mile,
> Until we found the bridge;
> Then past the hollow, o'er the stream
> And up onto the ridge.
>
> Sought high and low, paced here, paced there,
> Found one, then two, three, four,
> The rain fell hard, the cold wind blew,
> But still we searched for more.
>
> Soon five, then six. The chase was on,
> Now who would win the day?
> – The man, I think, whoe'er he was,
> Who stole the last away!

Except for friendly rivalry at least this husband and wife team were in perfect agreement, and in fact I have not heard that addiction to letterboxing have ever actually led to divorce or murder (though in fact one letterboxer did murder his wife, but I have been assured that an addiction to the moor was not a contributory cause). However, I am sure that many couples will have arrived back at their cars wrapped in a cold silence after a particularly bad day. Janet Goodson expresses the feelings of many in her poem.

I've tramped all day over rugged Dartmoor.
My legs are aching, my feet are quite sore.
I've jumped over streams that were much too wide,
All to look for a box with a stamp inside.

I tell myself that it can be fun,
As I lag behind my husband and son.
I do enjoy it I must admit,
And its keeping me strong, and healthy and fit.

But why when I'm ready to call it a day
Does he talk of another one not far away?
It's then you may hear me moan and exclaim –
That sometimes, this is a BLOODY daft game!

Well anyone who has stood in the middle of the moor, rain pouring down a chink in one's defences, hungry, cold, and hampered with a whining child or shivering dog will know that feeling. Yet given a beautiful day, a new box with a rather special stamp, and troubles are forgotten. One is hooked all over again!

Chapter 8

What is it about Dartmoor that makes it so special? Why should so many people become hooked to the magic of the moor? Perhaps it is not the same thing for everyone, what grabs one person may leave another quite unaffected, but there is a certain air of mystery that even the most unimaginative person seems to feel whenever they are on the open moor. You can even feel it when you drive on some of the more lonely and open roads. I have never driven over Dartmoor in a coach, but I like to think that even the tourists driving through on the way to a cream tea at Princetown find a little of the magic rubs off on them.

Perhaps the special aura is the result of human habitation over the centuries. A modern housing estate contains no ghosts, ancient settlements abound in them. Roman legions march on Hadrian's Wall, Monmouth's troops haunt the marshy plains of Sedgemoor and Ann Boleyn walks the walls of the Tower of London. On the whole the ghosts of Dartmoor are not so tangible, mostly it is just a "feeling". When Joshua Slocum became the first man to sail alone round the world, he wrote in his log of a "phantom helmsman", another being who was with him on his voyage, a sailor from times gone before. So it may be on Dartmoor. There may not be a human, or human habitation in sight, yet somehow you are alone but not lonely. Chattering crowds may get a hint of moorland magic, but on your own it becomes an almost solid thing, the atmosphere is so dense you could nearly reach out and touch it.

Boxes can commemorate people, events, or even a car!

Dartmoor has been inhabited for a very long time. When the Ice Ages receded, and the climate warmed up our early Bronze Age forebears colonised the moor, and though at first they built no homes that left any remains, the houses they built for the dead can still be seen. When you consider that the chambered tomb at Corringdon Ball was 140 feet long on completion, that is proof of a large and settled community. In the days before JCBs (or spades for that matter), a mound of earth and rock of that dimension must have taken a lot of people and a lot of man-hours to complete.

In the later Bronze Age the moor must have been one of the busiest areas in Britain. All over the Southern Moor one comes across stone rows, stone circles, hut circles and enclosures. By the Iron Age it is reckoned that within a half mile radius of Postbridge 1,000 people were living, a staggering thought when you think of the size of Postbridge today.

Had these people lived in the lower valleys or the coastal belt then the remains of their habitation would have long ago been buried under concrete, or been scattered by generations of ploughing, and their ghosts would become as scattered as their artifacts. But on Dartmoor things stay as they were left, like the ring-road they are allowed to fall into "benign disrepair", so a stone placed by man in a certain position 5,000 years ago may still be in that position today. Dartmoor is in fact a gigantic time capsule.

If the majority of ghosts only exist as a feeling, or a sensation, there are others that make themselves more noticed. Cadover Bridge is a popular picnic spot, and an area that gets crowded with tourists on summer Sundays. But "cad" is Celtic for battle, and on dark misty nights the shouts and cries of battle can sometimes still be heard. Above Lustleigh Cleave, where a Roman fort once stood the ghosts of Celts and Romans still make war today.

Across Dartmoor is an ancient track – the Lych Way, the road of the dead. Before Bishop Branscombe, Bishop of Exeter in the 13th Century, gave permission for the dead to be buried in Widecombe churchyard, all those who died on Dartmoor had to be carried to Lydford for burial. Ghostly funeral parties

Remains of the Chambered Tombe at Corringdon Ball.

have been seen ever since, threading their way through the mists, a coffin carried high in the middle of a solemn procession.

Not all Dartmoor ghosts are human. One of the best known animal ghosts is a black pony who haunts the area round Cranmere Pool. His name is Benjie, and he did start life as a human, in fact as Benjamin Gear, Mayor of Okehampton in the 17th Century, who – when caught sheep stealing – was condemned to empty Cranmere Pool with a sieve. A job he would seem to have successfully completed since there is no longer any water there – though perhaps other factors may have something to do with the drying up of the pool!

Perhaps one of the most unusual ghosts to haunt the moor is a sow and a family of piglets. They are seen in the area of the Walla Brook between Merripit Hill and Cator Gate trotting along in a search for food, and as they never succeed in finding any they get thinner and thinner. Why they should haunt the moor no one seems to know, most ghosts seem to have a reason for being where they are. The Raven, known as the Guardian of Chaw Gully, is said to be protecting a seam of gold in the old Birch Tor mine. He seems to be doing his job well as no one has so far been able to locate any gold!

A hare seen on the moor may, or may not, be what it seems. Dartmoor Witches specialise in turning themselves into these otherwise harmless animals, so if you do see a hare when you are alone on a bleak part of the moor it would be as well to cross your fingers just in case – you never know. Of course there are other ways of dealing with undesirable Dartmoor creatures. Did you know that if an adder should be blocking your path, all you have to do is draw a circle round it and the adder will be unable to move? I can't speak from personal experience on that one so I don't promise that it works, but it might be worth a try.

Dartmoor is a giant time capsule, Stone Rows at Merrivale.

Chapter 9

However lonely the moor may seem, you are sharing it not only with ghosts and other humans, but with a multitude of assorted creatures. Adders, being by nature shy, are rarely seen, and even more rare is a report of anyone being bitten by one. Dogs are likely to be in more danger than humans, and it is advisable to keep dogs on a lead if you think adders are likely to be about.

Probably the most potentially dangerous animal on the moor is a Galloway cow with a calf. If you meet cows with young calves when you are out on letterbox forays, it pays to give them a fairly wide berth – especially if you have a dog with you. The Dartmoor ponies will not stay to challenge you, should you disturb a herd they are likely to move off before you get too close. These days they are seldom true Dartmoor ponies, they are mostly crossbreeds, sometimes a mixture of Dartmoor and Shetland. The pure Dartmoor is more likely to be kept safe on its owner's farm. There have been ponies on the moor since they were introduced by the Celts in around 200 B.C., and the Romans were impressed by the West Country charioteers and their tough little ponies.

Just as it is with the true Dartmoor pony, so it is with the Dartmoor sheep. The traditional Devon Longwool, the Grayface and the Dartmoor are not often seen running on the open moor, a sheep more commonly seen is the Scottish Blackface.

True Dartmoor Ponies are seldom seen on the moor.

While on the subject of sheep and ponies, or for that matter cattle, I would like to point out what dangerous lives these animals lead. To start with, the roads are hazardous. Letterboxers "do it on foot", but nearly everyone has driven to the moor by car (and nearly everyone has probably driven there much too fast). The most potentially dangerous time for the animals is in late spring and summer, when the young are still with their mothers. You may slow down to let a mare cross the road, but did you think that her foal may be coming out of the bracken at a gallop 20 yards behind her? An apparently soporific sheep may at any minute get to her feet and decide – followed by her lambs – that the grass the other side of the road is greenest. The "Do Not Feed The Ponies" signs are not put there to spoil your children's fun, but to protect the ponies. Ponies fed near roads are going to hang about by the roadside, ponies that get tit-bits from people in cars are going to walk towards cars in the hope of getting more goodies. DON'T DO IT.

There is a very good organisation, called The Dartmoor Livestock Protection Society, and should you have the misfortune to be involved in an accident concerning livestock on the moorland roads, they will guarantee payment for the initial veterinary assistance for the animal involved. The telephone numbers of some local veterinary practices are at the end of this chapter.

Letterboxers, and all Dartmoor walkers, can also be of great assistance to sick or injured animals on the moor. Most of us feel that we would like to do something if we find an animal in a distressed condition, but how many know what is best? A great many farmers run their stock on the moor so how do you know who-to-report-what-to? Once again The Dartmoor Livestock Protection Society will help. If you come across, sheep, ponies or cattle collapsed, sick, injured or trapped, then ring South Brent 2174, or Buckfastleigh 43411 or Plymouth 556028. Of course it will help them if you can give them as many details as possible, so try to make a note of exactly where the animal is, and what it looks like – and for sheep especially the markings should be noted. Don't be fooled though if you

Dartmoor ponies, a Dartmoor witch, and a creature to be avoided – a sheep tick!

find a young lamb apparently "abandoned", nine times out of ten the lamb has only been "parked" by its mother while she goes off to graze, the lamb in need of urgent attention is the one you may find standing beside its *dead* mother. Remember – animals on the moor have a tough time, so in this way you can help them. Another point (obvious as it may seem) is PLEASE keep dogs under control. There is plenty of moor for everyone, let the livestock enjoy their life there in peace.

One last point while talking about livestock on the moor. Have you ever thought of letterboxing on horseback? Certainly one of the best ways to see the moor is from the back of a horse. Four legs seem to cover the ground so much easier than two, it seems a super idea. Be warned though, a certain letterboxing lady thought she would ride on a boxhunting trip. All went well till she got off to sign in at the box. There are not many places where you can tie a pony securely in the middle of the moor, and the result was that her pony went home without her. So unless you carry a tethering stake, or have someone with you to hold ponies while you hunt boxes, I don't think I would recommend it!

D.L.P.S. Road Casualties Emergency Aid.

The Society guarantees payment for initial veterinary assistance called to livestock road casualties by any member of the public or police force. The following telephone numbers of veterinary practices may prove useful.

Vaughan, Sanders, Warren and Brown .... Tavistock 2561
Claydon, Young and Harris .... Okehampton 2148
J. Edwards .... Ivybridge 2700
Parkinson and Watson .... Plymouth 51522
R. J. and V. E. Lowries .... Lydford 315
R. C. C. Piggott .... Moretonhampstead 441
and Bovey Tracey 833023
N. Bowden .... Yelverton 854255
Major J. D. Parkinson .... Yelverton 853145
A. K. Rumford .... Bovey Tracey 833310

... a sheep more commonly seen is the Scottish Blackface.

Chapter 10

There is no doubt that most dogs enjoy letterboxing with their owners, in fact what dog could not appreciate a hike over beautiful Dartmoor? Perhaps dogs find it a bit boring though, while their master or mistress searches a small area on hands and knees for a well hidden box, or take a particularly long time to sign in, so with this in mind we put out a letterbox for dogs. (I did warn you that letterboxers tended to be a trifle eccentric – didn't I?)

We have a very small Yorkshire Terrier called Mouse, and though – like her owners – she is getting a bit stiff in the joints, she does enjoy a letterbox walk. So Mouse put out a box for dogs, on Hound Tor of course. The box was placed under a tree so that dogs could leave their calling cards. The stamp has a picture of Mouse, and a visitors book for dogs' paw-prints, (there is also a visitors book for humans), a bag of dog-biscuits is provided so that dogs can have a small snack while waiting for their owners to sign in. Mouse then sent out some postcards to dogs that she knew walked with their owners, and so a new box was established.

Paw-prints of assorted sizes soon began to appear in the book, as dogs brought their owners to the box. First in the book was Bruce who claimed to have found the box on his own;

Petra, on the next page, said that she had to enlist the help of her owners as she couldn't read the compass. Nearly every page said "thanks for the biscuit", though one or two comments were not so appreciative. On one page was written "Blackberry and Tipsy. We haven't got a dog so we signed for our rabbits, but they don't like dog biscuits". A rather curious square paw-print was accompanied by the comment "Thanks for the biscuits, but I'm into silicon chips – K 9." Perhaps the most surprising entry was, "To Mouse the Dartmoor dog from Wallaby and Sheba, the cross-country cats." As this was accompanied by actual cat paw-prints, I hoped I would meet them one day.

The smallest paw-print in the book (other than Mouse's own), was that left by Tag, her Chihuahua boy friend, but some of the prints were so large that they hardly fitted on the page. William and Edward Basset from Sussex had very big feet as did Barney the Old English Sheepdog and Rebecca the Rottweiler. One page was completely filled up with the (appropriately) red paw-prints of Sasha, Heidi, Lisa and Penny, the four red-setters who walked the moors together. Of course the weather affected the quality of the prints, in wet weather we got some pretty odd smudges, and on a really snowy day the following comment was written in the book, "Could not bring my Yorkie, balls of snow the size of peaches on her breeches!!"

Occasionally the box runs out of biscuits before we can get out to Hound Tor to top it up, then sad little comments get written in the book. Such as:- "No biscuit for Sam, he will need a special supper tonight", and "NO BISCUITS, but he had two last time!" Once a visitor, who always signs in to boxes as Old Maid wrote the following:-

The Old Maid (not Hubbard)
Went to the cupboard
To get her poor dog a biscuit.
When she got there
The box it was bare
So she came back next day just to fix it!

She did too, the box was topped up, and no more dogs were disappointed.

One or two dogs never reached the box but their owners entered into the spirit of fun and wrote in the book for them. One left the comment:- "Holly, the Cocker Spaniel, had puppies a week ago so was unable to come (I've taken a biscuit home for her, thank-you!)." Pedro of the Beechfielders got there though, he left a paw-print to prove it and the following note:- "Blind and diabetic, but still made it! Thank you Mousey."

In the book for humans, I suggested that if anyone did not have a "personal stamp" to sign in the book with, they might like to leave a thumb-print. A lot of people did this, and it was amusing to see, by the size of thumb-prints, the ages of the visitors to the box. Several two year olds have been there, and one family left five prints in assorted sizes. Granny, Mum, Dad, Tristan (age 6) and Tamsin (age 2). They also wrote the comment:- "We all feel very silly now, we've all got blue thumbs!" But such is the spirit of "Mouse's Box" that I don't expect they really minded.

Mouse (and her owner) stamping up at "Mouse's Box".

Chapter 11

Mouse is not the only dog to have a box put out in her honour, there have in fact been several, and one or two dedicated to other animals. Unfortunately most of the animal boxes are put out in memory of what was a much loved pet, and the fronts of some of the visitors books can make sad reading.

"Tinker's Bridge" was put out in memory of Tinker, a cat, and Fred, another cat has a box in his memory at Hameldown. But perhaps the saddest box of all is "Annie's Song", near Combestone Tor. This box was put out in memory of Annie, a long-haired Dachshund, who met with a sad accident on the moor, and Christine Parsons wrote the following poem in her honour:-

Stamps from "Mouse's Box" and others –

Annie, oh my Annie!
After I had waved farewell to Pat,
Before I turned away, I saw you,
Dancing at her heels,
Delighted at the promise of a walk....
Had I known then,
I would have called and kept you by my side,
Despite the disappointment in your eyes;
But if Fate does not spare human lives,
How much less one small dog?
Ten Tors training;
The rain poured down; the haversacks weighed heavily;
Burdened with poles and tents, appliances and gear.
Some could not bear them,
And others took their share, to lighten heavy loads.
The rain poured down; the going was hard,
With footholds wet and muddy ... then the stream,
Swollen to a torrent,
The boulders, lichen-covered, slippery and false....
The weighty haversack took toll of balance,
She slipped and fell,
And you, my Annie, following obediently to heel,
Were crushed between the granite and unyielding poles.
The rain poured down; and mingled with the tears,
As they carried you to me; and I wept,
To see my little Annie lie so still, and realised
No more would you come running to my call.
The rain poured down; as we took you to the woods,
To find a final resting-place.
The keeper thought us poachers, as we stepped,
Hooded and silently, along the path,
But when he saw our burden, knew our pain,
For he had lost his dog quite recently;
He showed us where you might lie undisturbed
By flood or weather, and he dug your grave.
So I laid you in, with face wet, but not from rain,
And left you with a lullaby of winds,
Amongst the small creatures of the glade,
Whose gentle footfalls shall be your company.
Annie, my Annie, rest you well,
My little dog, I shall not forget you.

And of course Annie is not forgotten, and though Annie Mark 2 is doing her best to fill the hole left in her owner's heart, somewhere, the ghost of a little Dachshund still hunts rabbits over the moor. Probably with much the same excitement that humans hunt for the letterbox put out in her honour!

Griff, who has a box put out in his memory at Grippers Hill lived to a ripe old age, the visitors book at his box tells us that he died on August 9th 1985, aged 15 years. Heidi, has the distinction of even having a cross in her memory, near Crazywell Pool, but they are just a few of the dogs remembered in boxes. Among the live dogs to have a box are Blue and Monty, two police dogs from Princetown, who had the distinction of sharing a box at Cowsic Head.

One of the more unlikely animal boxes was put out in memory of a goat. "Lara", an Anglo-Nubian matron has a box in her honour on Pu Tor, put out by the rest of the Buckator Herd (with a little assistance from their owner Siobhan Peters). Tottie, Lara's daughter, Coco, her grand-daughter, Kalmia, Hannah and Gemma can look out from their home near Tavistock to the part of the moor where Lara is remembered; and as new arrivals to the goat herd are recorded in the visitors book, letterboxers can keep up to date with any births in the Buckator herd. A charming touch, and all part of the "letterbox lunacy" that people can enjoy on the moors!

Chapter 12

It seems perfectly natural for dogs to enjoy walking on Dartmoor – whether hunting for letterboxes, or accompanying their owners on any other expedition. Dogs are man's oldest companion, and are to be found all over the globe. From Eskimo sled dogs, to African herd dogs and on to the sleeve dogs of Peking – dogs in varying shapes and sizes have accompanied their masters since the days of pre-history.

Paintings of dogs have been found on cave walls alongside spear throwing hunters, chasing the extinct aurochs; and statues of the dog Nubis guarded the 3,000 year old tombs of the ancient Pharaohs. In more recent times, the terrier, "Bothie", literally travelled "to the Ends of the Earth" with Randolph Fiennes' Transglobe Expedition in 1979–82, and before man ventured into space, the Russian dog "Laika" orbited the earth.

So, as I say, dogs on Dartmoor seems perfectly natural, but cats? That is another matter. But, as mentioned before, two cats had signed their paw-prints into the book at Mouse's Box, so – highly intrigued – we tried to find out more about them. They turned out to be two enchanting Siamese, and after a few letters had passed between them and Mouse, they agreed to meet us on Bone Hill Rocks to be photographed. Not the easiest of assignments, the cats were in their element, dashing up and down the rocks, hiding in cat-sized caves and popping out of holes that seemed too small for a squirrel. It takes a brave owner to let a cat run loose on a vast expanse like Dartmoor, but the Whites confidence in "Wallaby" and "Sheba" was fully

The cats were in their element, dashing up and down the rocks....

justified. They are more obedient than many dogs, and when called, came galloping down the slope, ready to go home again in the car. Before they went home we introduced them to Mouse, but though they seem to like most things, that does not include dogs!

If you think hunting for letterboxes with two free-range cats is brave (or mad), what would you think to walking the moors with a hen? Believe it or not that is just what Brenda, a keen letterboxer used to do, and Jason used to be a familiar sight, hopping along behind her owner. If Jason seems an odd name for a hen, I would ask if you have ever tried to sex a fluffy little yellow chick – it takes a real expert. So the name was not really surprising, nor was Jason surprising to look at, just an ordinary sort of backyard brown hen, but when it came to walking – Jason was very special.

She really did go everywhere, and on her own two feet, with an occasional flap of her wings if she got left behind. She was such a capable walker that I wouldn't have been surprised if she had carried her own tiny back-pack! However, she had no need to as Brenda always carried a suitable "hen lunch" for her (dry corn in case of accidents if lunch was to be eaten in a pub). When I met Brenda and Jason out walking one day, we introduced Mouse and Jason. Because Jason was scared of dogs, Mouse was introduced as a "nice cat", whether this reassured her, or whether she just thought Mouse was too small to be scared of I wouldn't know, but they accepted each other and walked down the path together.

Sadly, her fear of dogs was justified, and it was a dog that caused her demise. Brenda has had other hens – but there will never be another Jason.

Of other furry friends who walk the moors, probably the best known is "Survival Teddy", who walked with Juliette his owner, and at one time even carried his own travelling box and stamp with him. "Heathcliffe", who came from a "home for battered hedgehogs", is a hedgehog glove puppet owned by two restauranteers from Avebury. He has not missed a letterboxing hunt yet, and endorses the point that though you don't have to be mad to enjoy letterboxing, it does help!

Jason out letterboxing.

Chapter *13*

What do you do if you are a "letterbox nut-case" and the rest of the family are not? Or conversely, Mum, Dad, boyfriend, Uncle Tom Cobley and all are letterbox hunters, and the very idea bores you stiff? The answer is simple, do your own thing. After all there are 365 square miles of Dartmoor, so there is space for everyone to do something different.

First, for the semi-active. Hunting for an ammunition tin put out on the moor last week, does not necessarily grab everybody, so before setting off on an expedition – sit down and study the map. The new 1:25,000 Outdoor Leisure Map is excellent, though failing that the Dartmoor Tourist Map will do. We will take for an example the area around Dartmeet, real "grockel" country, but none the less, a beautiful spot. Grannie and her knitting can be parked near the river, to enjoy the sounds and sight of the East Dart as it flows under the remains of the clapper bridge. For an enjoyable walk on the flat, she and Grand-dad can follow the river upstream, the ancient hamlet at Babeny is particularly beautiful. The tiny clapper bridge on the path was once the only means for pedestrians heading for Huccaby direction. In the opposite direction from Dartmeet one can cross the West Dart by the stepping stones, and follow the footpath either way.

The Coffin Stone.

Ancient history lovers in the party can have a field day. The area above Badger's Holt is thick with hut circles, some of which are very large and still well defined. Most of them are quite close to the road, and in the triangle between Yar Tor and the cross roads at the top of Dartmeet hill lie the remains of a settlement. Also at the crossroads is Ouldsbroom Cross, or rather what is left of it, unfortunately it had its arms cut off and was used for many years as a gate post at Town Farm, Luesdon before being rescued and re-erected in the 1950s. On the way back down the hill to Dartmeet, take a small detour from the road and you will find the Coffin Stone. This is the stone on which, traditionally, the bearers could put the coffin while they rested on the long sad walk to Widecombe Church. Funeral parties must, by necessity, have been large in the days before roads enabled a horse-drawn hearse to make the journey, even the strongest bearer could not carry a coffin far in that sort of terrain. If you have any problem finding the Coffin Stone I can only advise that it is about three-quarters of the way down the hill from Poundsgate on the left, and is the one with crosses and initials on it. History does not tell us whether these were carved by pall bearers during a break, or whether someone carved them afterwards in memory of a loved one, but as I can't imagine the mourners being equipped with a hammer and chisel at such a time – I suspect it was the latter.

While the rest of the family is enjoying the delights of Dartmeet and its surrounds, our letterbox enthusiast should have quite a bit of time to go off box-hunting. I am not going to tell anyone exactly where to go to look for boxes, for, with the exception of the few on the Ordnance Survey map, the positions are not permanent, and boxes come and go; but at the time of writing there are several within a mile radius of the area, so a good time should be had by all. Almost every area of Dartmoor has something to interest everyone, so if you are a family with differing interests – use your map, use your head, and keep everyone happy.

Even non-walkers should be able to find plenty to keep them occupied while their "other half" hunts boxes. How about taking some binoculars along, and taking up bird-watching?

Where could you find a more beautiful place to do a spot of painting? Or how about collecting lists of flowers seen on your walk? Or Lichens? Mosses? Or Mineral samples? The possibilities are endless. (Please remember though that wild flowers are protected, so don't come off the moor with an armfull of rare orchids!)

Even if you are a complete "non-boxer", it could well pay you to go along on a box hunting trip. Let the dedicated letterboxers go about on their hands and knees hunting for ammunition boxes and the like – you can just enjoy yourself. While they are getting fraught with their heads to the ground – take a look about you – isn't Dartmoor a wonderful place; and letterboxers really do get to the parts that others can't reach. Who knows? After a few trips out to the centre of the moor you might even find yourself addicted – YOU HAVE BEEN WARNED!

Chapter 14

One aspect of box-hunting few could fail to enjoy is visiting some of the pubs on the moor that now have a box. Who could resist the idea of getting a nice new stamp and signing the visitors book while sitting in front of a roaring log fire, drink in hand, while the elements do their worst outside.

To the purist this may not be strictly letterboxing, but in its own way it can be great fun. The first hostelry to have a box was the Plume of Feathers at Princetown, and the idea of a "pub box" was thought up by the landlord James Langton and his friends. Princetown is strategically placed almost in the centre of the moor and walkers have always been made welcome at the Plume. Muddy boots and dripping clothes are never frowned on, and letterboxers, parties of "yomping" marines, off-duty prison warders and tidy folk from Plymouth can mingle in the bar. The stamp is kept in a red Pillar-Box and the visitors book is well into the fourth edition. At one time there was a Dartmoor letterbox known as "Hollow Bottom" that no one seemed able to find. A minute search of the Survey map, Crossing's Guide and Hemery's "High Dartmoor" failed to produce any reference to such a place. Eventually, one day, someone dropped the Plume box on the floor, surprise, surprise, the box had a hollow bottom and a tiny stamp and visitors book appeared. Another Dartmoor letterbox puzzle was solved.

…The only time of year when letterboxing becomes impossible is when the snow is really thick….

The Forest Inn at Hexworthy has for some years been very involved with the letterboxing fraternity. It was here that the first Dartmoor Walkers and Letterboxers Bi-annual Get-Togethers were held. These were organised by Morton Smith-Petersen, and held on the Sundays that started or ended British Summertime (or clock-change days as they are known to letterboxers). A new stamp is produced for each meeting, and the first visitors book is now completely filled and has been presented to the Museum of Dartmoor life at Okehampton. From the first get-together, which was attended by about 150 people, numbers have risen each time, and now about 1,000 call in at some time during the day. Regretfully, the venue has had to be changed as the Forest Inn was not designed for such a crowd, but there is a permanent letterbox behind the bar, so the connection with letterboxing is still maintained.

Quite a few other pubs within the Dartmoor National Park also have introduced a letterbox, and though I have no doubt that it brings in quite a lot of custom if there is a nice stamp to be gained, it can also give a welcome break to a weary letterboxer, and the standard of stamps is very high. One pub, The King's Arms in Okehampton, entered into the letterboxing spirit by producing an original clue when their box first came out. Hunters were told to:- "Take a regal step back in time, and from a granite post next to St. James' Chapel, go 40 paces on a bearing of 121° to the royal lounge. Then 9 paces 321° to the box." If followed correctly these directions brought one right up to the bar counter!

Probably the only time of year when letterboxing becomes impossible is when the snow is really thick on the moors. A great many box clues have directions such as "...under long granite boulder with grass on top ... look for 2' slanting stone at end of clitter" etc. Not too difficult under ordinary conditions, but under three feet of snow everything looks the same, you could be standing above the rock in question and not be aware of it. However, thanks to the innovation of "pub letterboxes", as long as the roads are passable, you can collect letterbox stamps in any weather conditions – though you might have to wait for opening time!

Chapter 15

You may think that letterboxers are a strange lot, but there is something about Dartmoor that brings out the latent eccentricity in everyone.

As Jack Follows wrote in the Jack Knight Air Log and AFA News ... "Dartmoor is a place where anything can happen, and usually does! Some of you may recall how in the recent past a Mormon missionary was kidnapped and held as an (unwilling) sex-slave by an American blonde-bombshell, in a lonely cottage on the moor. Even stranger – he complained! ..."

This air of oddness is reflected in some of the strange industries that have flourished – or floundered – on the moor. Take for example raspberry growing. Would you have thought that raspberries would prosper on the North Moor? Actually, I don't think they did, but a certain Mr. Brock tried to grow them in a hollow at Watern Combe. The only thing left to remind us of his efforts today is the name "Raspberry Garden", and there was at one time a letterbox of that name in the area.

Most of the other odd ventures that have been tried out (and for one reason or another failed) have been commemorated by the letterboxers. For example, the Ice Works at Sourton. On the face of it this seemed a good idea; the area is plenty cold enough for the manufacture of ice during the winter months, and there was a demand for ice for the Plymouth fishing industry. But of course the days before refrigerators were invented were also the days before motor vehicles and good roads, and whereas ice will keep for a very long time in a pit on the North Moor, it will not stand the long wagon journey from Sourton to Plymouth. What started as big blocks of ice would have reached the fish market as ice cubes!

Did you know that gunpowder was made of ground up sulphur, salpetre and charcoal? In 1844 a powder mill was built on Dartmoor, about two miles North-East of Two Bridges, to fill the demand for blasting at the many tin mines then working on the moor. The remains of the chimney and many of the buildings can still be seen, and the mortar used to test powder is still in position at the end of the drive. There must at one time have been quite a community there, as in addition to the many houses built for the workmen, there was also a dame school and a chapel. The workmen's houses were not (as is usual) terraced, but were detached, so that should one be blown up by accident they would not all fall down!

This was one of Dartmoor's more thriving industries, but unfortunately for those who worked there, Doctor Alfred Nobel invented dynamite in 1867 and the demand for gunpowder declined. In the 1880s Powder Mills closed, another Dartmoor industry that had a short career.

The definition of glass in the Concise Oxford Dictionary, starts as follows:- "Substance, usu. transparent, lustrous, hard and brittle, made by fusing sand with soda or potash or both and other ingredients...." Note the words "usually transparent", because it was largely the lack of transparency in the glass that led to the failure of the glass works at Meldon.

In the 1880s a vein of granulite was discovered in a quarry at Meldon Gorge, close to the viaduct. A glass works was started near-by, specialising in small bottles for the pharmaceutical trade, but as the glass was a semi-opaque blueish-green it did not find much of a market. Today all that remains is the quarry, where several veins of granulite can still be seen (in addition to

Ruins at Powder Mills.

a fine display of mosses), and the remains of some buildings where you may pick up pieces of the distinctive coloured glass. This brave try at a Dartmoor industry has not been overlooked by the letterboxers, and many collections will have the glass works stamp in.

In these days of Myxomatosis in rabbits, does it seem a sensible idea to keep masses of wild rabbits in a man-made warren? Actually this was one of Dartmoor's more sensible industries, and one that flourished from Norman times till comparatively recently. In the days before silage and compound feeds, a great many of the cattle and sheep were slaughtered and salted down at the onset of winter. In the days when meat and bread were the staple diet, a nice fresh rabbit must have meant a welcome addition to a boring menu. Rabbits were transported from the moor to Plymouth, Tavistock and other Devon towns; the usual mode of transport being by pack-horse. Probably the oldest recorded warren was Trowlsworthy, on the South Moor. It was granted to Sampson de Traylesworthy before 1272, but there is still plenty there to see today, and the pillow mounds and kennel field are well preserved.

In his definition of a warren, Crossing states that "...like a forest and a chase, a warren was land set apart for the preservation of game, and the beasts and birds of the warren were the hare and the coney, the pheasant and the partridge. As a breeding place for rabbits alone there are several warrens on Dartmoor...." The importance of these warrens is stressed by the fact that the tinners' emblem was three rabbits, joined in a circle. These can be seen in a carving in Widecombe Church, and on the old sign of the Warren House Inn. In 1831, the Reverend Mr. Edward Atkyns Bray, then vicar of Tavistock, recorded the poem from the sign:-

> Here is cider and beer
> Your hearts for to cheer.
> And if you want meat
> To make up a treat,
> There are rabbits to eat.

Industries Ancient and Modern. Trowlsworthy Warren and Lee Moor China Clay Works.

Showing that the warrens were fully operational at this date. This same reverend gentleman and his wife are owed a debt of gratitude by all who are interested in the history of Dartmoor. He was almost the earliest of Dartmoor explorers, and although he was apt to credit the "Druids" with the responsibility for erecting the stone rows and circles on the moor, and thought that they – rather than the elements – were responsible for logan stones and rock basins, he discovered and listed more antiquities than anyone else before or since. He and his wife were prolific writers, and while her husband recorded all he could of the pre-history of the moor, Mrs. Bray collected many bits of moorland folklore that had been handed down solely by word of mouth for generations.

One industry, coming under the heading of unusual rather than odd, is peat cutting. Peat is the youngest of the world's fossil fuels, and therefore is nearest the surface and most easily obtainable. In the days of the tinners large amounts were cut to make charcoal, but now a peat cutter is a rare sight. One of the last men to cut peat on Dartmoor is also a letterboxer – not that this makes him a "nut-case", far from it, it makes good sense for anyone who has turbary rights on the moor to get their winter fuel free.

The only cost of peat (or "turf" as it is known on Dartmoor) is, of course, a lot of hard work coupled with the know-how. There is peat covering a large amount of Dartmoor, but to be of any use as a fuel the peat must be of the right kind and must be cut and dried in the right way at the right time of year, and with the right tools. Fred Ward, helped by his wife Joan spends a lot of time and energy in the summer months, cutting, drying and stacking peat, but his reward is a year's supply of fuel. What better end to a winter's day of letterboxing, than toasting oneself before a roaring peat fire?

... a peat cutter is a rare sight. Fred Ward at work.

Chapter 16

With the possible exception of the china clay workings in the Lee Moor area, the industry that has had the most impact on the moor is the tin industry. Letterboxing makes one conversant with some odd snippets of information, and words such as:- leat, launder (no connection with clothes washing!), wheel-pit, tail-race, cache, blowing house, stamping mill, mould stone, etc. are part of everyday letterbox language. The reason being, of course that there is often a box hidden near a mining site. Though I would stress that boxes must NEVER be hidden actually in sites of historical interest, so please, please do not disturb any tinners' artifacts. Nearly every named mine on the moor has (or has had) a box put out in its honour, at the time of writing there are boxes near Vitifer Mine, Golden Dagger Mine, Wheal Betsy, Wheal George, Wheal Jewel and Wheal Katherine. Boxes come and go, but it is a fact that most interesting sites on Dartmoor now have a letterbox nearby.

One keen letterboxer even went so far as to smelt himself a small piece of tin by the old methods. It says a lot for his determination that he actually succeeded in producing a small ingot measuring $\frac{3}{4}'' \times \frac{1}{4}'' \times \frac{3}{16}''$ by methods even more primitive than that of the pre-industrial age smelters. For instance, when Ian was trying to crush the stone, he had to pound it by hand which was, to quote him, "a muscle wrenching task", at least the ancient tinners had water driven stamping mills. After much experimenting, tired muscles, a

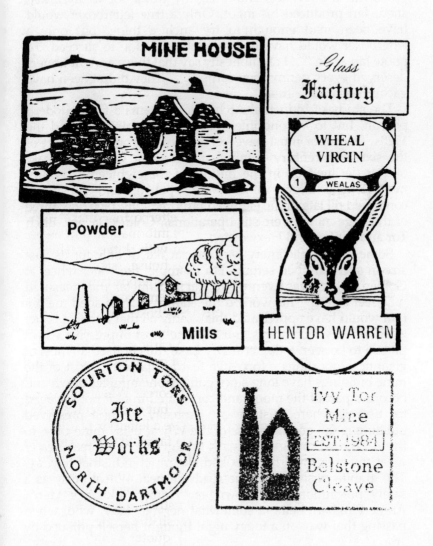

Some reminders of Dartmoor's industrial past–2.

worn out vacuum cleaner (this had provided the blowing power for the furnace) and a slightly worse for wear garden shed, Ian produced his ingot. Only a true letterboxer would have been mad enough to try such a thing, but only a letterboxer would have had the determination to succeed. To quote Ian again "... I can honestly say that those ancient tinners deserved every penny they earned...." They didn't even have vacuum cleaners either!

The study of Industrial Archaeology seems a fairly modern pursuit, but to anyone interested in such things around the 1920s, Dartmoor must have been Mecca. Around the start of the sixteenth century, mining on the moor was at its peak, output declined till in the middle of the eighteenth century most of the larger mines were opened, and prosperity continued till late in the eighteen hundreds. By 1900 only three of the large mines were still operational, Golder Dagger, Birch Tor and Vitifer, and Hexworthy.

Some of the machinery was spectacular, if only for its vast size in such an open setting. For example, the water wheel at Golden Dagger was twenty-two feet in diameter and measured nine feet across. This worked the stamps that crushed the ore (Ian would have appreciated this), sadly all that remains today is the pit in which it was housed. The most impressive wheel pit still to be seen today is at Dry Lake, this housed a wheel of gigantic proportions – forty-five feet in diameter. Most of the mine buildings have long since gone, stone tumbles down and becomes part of the moor, and corrugated iron, if not salvaged for use elsewhere, rusts away. Probably the best preserved building is the engine house of the Wheal Betsy mine close to the A386 road though this stark ruin gives one no real idea of what the area must have looked like in its industrial heyday. The granite posts, set at the roadside near Wheal Betsy as a safety precaution, are known as "Annie Pinkham's Men". Annie Pinkham being a somewhat nervous lady, who, when passing that way on a foggy night thought herself pursued by "men".

There is something about Dartmoor mists (or potent Devon cider?), that seems to give life to granite stones. The Grey

Wheal Betsy Mine.

Wethers, stone circles between Sittaford Tor and Fernworthy Forest was once sold to a gullible farmer as a "fine flock of grey wethers", it is not recorded what the farmer said when he went out to view his purchase in a good light!

One hears horrific tales of old time travellers being lost in the terrible mists of Dartmoor, and it was the proud boast of the prison authorities, some years ago, that no escaped convict had ever got off the moor. To those who do not know the moor it is easy to imagine a Rank/Disney type set, craggy rocks, bottomless mires and swirling mists, but though Dartmoor should always be treated with respect it is in no way a frightening place.

Like most other types of people, letterboxers can be sorted out into grades. A great number of them collect boxes from the more accessible areas, and some of the 100 Club members may never have walked more than half a mile from their cars. It is perfectly possible to collect boxes even if one is not a great walker, or if one has toddlers holding up one's progress. Others are more ambitious, and one family has reached some surprising places complete with daughter in her wheelchair! For the serious, addicted letterboxer, to reach the centre of the moor is essential, and though the fogs and bogs are not as bad as some would have us believe, they should still be treated with caution.

The secret of enjoying one's letterboxing, and not being a potential nuisance to others, is simple – as Baden Powell always advocated – "Be Prepared".

Letterboxing is a surprisingly time consuming occupation. What started as a quick half-day outing can extend into a marathon. A box that should have been easy to find, may take an hour or more of diligent searching, or at one box you may find news of another only a mile or two away. In the meantime, what started as a nice sunny day may well have turned into a cold, drizzly afternoon. No problem to the well equipped boxer, he simply dons his waterproofs, refreshes himself with the iron rations he always carries, and with the aid of his map and compass, finds first the box he is after, and then the shortest way back to his car.

Annie Pinkham's Men.

Chapter 17

Not everyone is interested in industrial archaeology, but it must be impossible to walk about Dartmoor hunting little boxes without finding something else of interest. The moor is a fascinating place.

For the wildlife lover there may not, at first sight, be a lot to see. Most of the mammals one is likely to find are of the domesticated variety, and even the rabbit – legacy of the warreners days – is no longer so common since the decimation from Myxomatosis severely reduced its numbers. Otters are very rare, and should anyone know where one may be seen, they are unlikely to let on. Deer are also an extreme rarity, though on occasion a straggler may wander over from Exmoor. The resident deer were hunted down by the Duke of Bedford's hounds in the eighteenth century. The last date on which a deer was officially reported killed by hounds on Dartmoor being 1780.

It is reckoned that there are four foxes to every square mile of Dartmoor, and several local hunts now keep them in check. Foxes seem to have suffered a population explosion, the first one recorded on the moor was in 1802, when the Reverend Mr. E.A. Bray found fox footprints at Cranmere Pool while he was out on one of his explorations. Another animal that has started to colonise the moor in very recent times is the mink, and the old Otter Hunt has now reformed into a mink hunting pack to try to keep these vicious little animals under control. Sometimes one may startle a sleeping fox on the open moor, contrary to popular belief, foxes sleep above ground for most of the year, but they do not move till almost tripped over, so seeing one is largely a matter of luck.

Badgers are commonly supposed to be woodland creatures, but it is difficult to take a walk on the Southern Moor without coming upon an active set. Badgers are great diggers, and the tunnels into the heart of the set may be ten or more feet long. All this digging naturally produces a lot of spoil, and it is this that one first notices when finding a set. In spring, when there may be cubs underground, old "bedding" may be seen dragged out of one of the holes – badgers are very clean creatures, and where there is an active set there will be a "latrine" for communal badger use, at a discreet distance.

Badgers and foxes have often featured on letterbox stamps. The box at Fox Tor is one of the original fifteen boxes that were on the moor in 1976, and though the book, the "Belstone Fox" features the Belstone in Leicestershire not the Dartmoor Belstone, there has also been a Belstone Fox stamp on the moor. Two of the most recent Badger boxes have been "Badgers at Avon" and "Badgers at play on Standon Hill".

Birdlife on Dartmoor is abundant and varied. In spring it is almost impossible to walk on the South Moor without hearing the incessant call of the cuckoo, so it is not surprising that one of the earliest boxes on the moor was put out at Cuckoo Rock. This box, being rather close to a "Grockel" frequented road, has suffered badly from vandals, but though the box site has been moved up a bit and down a bit, and the stamp has often had to be renewed, the box is still there, and from time to time there have been other boxes close by to keep it company.

There is a heron on the stamp at the box at Deep Swincombe; one might think this was an unlikely place for a heron to be, but oddly enough they are almost as common in the middle of the moor as up the Dart Estuary, one only has to remember that they are as partial to frogs and small water mammals as well as fish, to see why.

Several of the birds that can be seen on Dartmoor are rarities in other habitats, and a keen "twitcher" can often get a sighting of an unusual foreign visitor – bird visitor that is, not just an Australian tourist! Even the average walker, who keeps his eyes and ears open, will see plenty of the more unusual birds.

Grouse are relatively common, look for them near where heather (their main item of diet) grows, even if you do not actually see a grouse, you may well find their droppings in a patch of bare ground between heather clumps, or hear their cry:- "Go-bak, go-bak" as they fly off at your approach. Ravens nest on several areas of the moor, in spring they give wonderful aerobatic displays, even looping-the-loop and flying up-side-down for short distances. In the silence of the moor their croaks can often be heard as they fly overhead.

In summer, ring ouzels nest in the high moors. Looking like blackbirds with white bibs, they are shy, retiring birds, but can sometimes be spotted, perched on a rock, singing to their mate. Golden plovers, autumn and winter visitors, can be seen in large flocks. They too are shy, and are more likely to be spotted on the wing than on the ground. The dipper is unusual in that it may be seen underwater! This little bird is so aerodynamically (or should it be aquadynamically) shaped, that it is able to run along the bottom of fast flowing rivers in search of food, and it is seldom found far from water.

The wheatear is common on Dartmoor. Looking at these sparrow-sized little birds it seems hard to believe they were once considered a delicacy and that in Victorian times, vast numbers were trapped as they migrated to and from their northern breeding grounds.

With the abundance of bird-life on the moor, it is not surprising that there is also an abundance of "bird boxes". The Aviary box at Pu Tor has a beautiful stamp that prints out in multi-colours the bird it is currently depicting. There has been a robin, a starling, a chaffinch, a woodpigeon and a kingfisher. The Burrator Wildlife series on Peak Hill is not confined to birds as it has included an adder stamp and a hare in addition to the birds so far depicted.

Owls can be seen on the moor, both in nature and on

Dartmoor, Flora, Fauna and Phenomena.

stamps. The barn owl, a bird mainly found in farmland areas, has been seen hunting over the moor like a pale silent ghost, and the tawny owl will nest in the more wooded spots and can be heard calling at night. William Shakespeare confused centuries of bird spotters by describing the tawny owl's call as "Tu-whit Tu-whoo" – he got it wrong! Tawny owls either call "Hooo, hooo, hoo-oo-oo" or "Kee-wick, kee-wick" not both together. The Bard was obviously not a naturalist, but such was his influence over the English language that his description of the tawny owl's cry is seldom queried. The owl series of stamps, put out in various sites on the moor has depicted barn, tawny, eagle and snowy owls, but the box of that name is all you will see of the latter two as they are extremely rare visitors to this country. In fact the eagle owl has not been reported in Britain this century.

Probably the commonest bird of prey to be seen on Dartmoor is the buzzard, and there have been several boxes with buzzards on the stamp. Though often to be seen perching on a post, eyes swivelling in a perpetual search for small rodents, they are at their most spectacular as they soar over the moor with scarcely a wing flap. Their eyesight is so keen that they can spot a mouse moving from two hundred yards away, and when they land in pursuit of one they can run for a short distance with surprising speed and agility.

While on the subject of Dartmoor wildlife, I must mention an odd incident – so odd that it could only have happened to a letterboxer. The Wady family were out with their dogs on a box-hunting excursion at Skir Hill when their Shetland Sheepdog ran off in pursuit of an animal. This animal turned out to be a squirrel, and when Stephen was rescuing it from the dog, the ungrateful rodent bit him! Have you ever tried to explain to a doctor how you came by a nasty squirrel bite, in the middle of nowhere, and two miles from the nearest wood? No wonder letterboxers get a reputation for being "nut-cases". Mind you I think it must have been a squirrel "nut-case" as the Wady's were convinced it was living in a rabbit-hole! Just another case of Dartmoor eccentricity, even the animals seem to catch it.

BADGERS AT PLAY

ON STANDON HILL

HUNTED FOX

BAGGATOR

548806

Dartmoor Letterbox

BELSTONE TOR

FOX TOR COMBE

LANGCOMBE HEAD CAIRN

Badgers and foxes are quite common on Dartmoor.

Chapter *18*

Whether you simply go letterboxing for letterboxing's sake, or whether you do a little birdwatching, antiquity hunting or whatever on the side, there is a certain magic about Dartmoor that grabs one sooner or later, and even the most hardened letterboxer cannot fail to come under the spell of the moor. If letterboxing is an addictive sport, then Dartmoor is an addictive place.

Every beautiful place has its devotees, but Dartmoor more than most. Of the many hundreds of letters Godfrey receives each year in connection with the 100 Club, nearly everyone says how letterboxing has opened their eyes to new aspects of the moor, and has taken them to places they had never visited before – or that they had never dreamed existed. People who have visited Dartmoor on a childhood holiday never quite forget it, a great many come back on a return visit as adults and become hooked on the moor (and letterboxing). As one addict wrote in her letter – "What did we do before letterboxing?"

Some of the abundant "bird boxes".

Luckily not everyone has the same "favourite place" on Dartmoor, or one area might tend to become excessively crowded. To everyone their choice, whether it is the vast expanses of blanket peat on the North Moor, the beautiful Dart Valleys of the central plain, or the rocky Tors and ancient remains of the South Moor, there is something for everyone.

Some people rush about madly from box to box, determined to stop at nothing in their haste to gain the prestige of a 100 Club badge, then a 500 badge or a 1,000 badge. They must always try to be first in every new visitors book at every new box, and take their letterboxing very seriously. Others take life at a leisurely pace, enjoy the wonderful scenery of the moor, and collect a letterbox stamp or two during the course of an afternoon's ramble.

Both get just as much fun out of their letterboxing, it is a game that can be enjoyed in a multitude of ways – there are no rules except for the Code of Conduct, which applies only to letterboxers, and the Country Code, which applies to all who walk, drive or ride on anyone else's land. One must never forget that, though Dartmoor is a National Park, all the land is privately owned, and to walk on it is a privilege not to be abused.

Some of us may find it hard to say just why they find walking on Dartmoor so special; an American letterboxer put it in words:-

(1) It's harder.
(2) It's big enough so we can always be alone.
(3) It seems less polluted than other places.
(4) We see so many birds, insects and flowers.
(5) It has made us give up eating lamb – FOR EVER.
(6) We are learning so much geography, geology and history painlessly.
(7) Letterboxing!

I doubt if letterboxing inspires the majority of its devotees to turn vegetarian! But in other respects, I am sure most letterboxers would agree with her – Dartmoor is a wonderful place. If you are thinking of starting letterboxing, be warned, it really is addictive, but if you do decide to have a go, or if you are a letterboxer already – GOOD HUNTING – and remember the rules:-

Now come all ye walkers
Who wander the moor,
From the depths of Dart Valley
To the heights of Yes Tor.
From the bogs of Raybarrow
To the banks of the Taw,
All walkers should know
And comply with the law.

Wear all the right gear
Take a compass and map.
A professional approach
Can forstall a mishap.
Keep your boxes away
From the huts and stone rows,
Let historical Dartmoor
Enjoy its repose.

In the war against litter
Let's have no respite,
And letterbox owners
Clear out your old sites.
Help preserve Dartmoor
Maintain our good name,
'Cause when all's said and done –
"It's only a game".

Thanks, "El Hombre", that is good letterboxing in a nutshell!

Since 1986, when "More Dartmoor Letterboxes" was first printed, some things have inevitably changed, though letterboxing itself continues as "madly" as ever. Please see overleaf for alterations.

Unfortunately the cost of badges has had to keep pace with inflation, so the price of the "100 Club Badge" mentioned on page 27 is now £1.50, but the good news is that there IS now a 5,000 badge (see page 29).

Sadly, pets have short lives, and "Mouse" and many of her canine friends are now in the "Great Kennel in the Sky". Though they will never be forgotten, we welcome all the new four-legged Letterbox Hounds who walk the moors with their owners.

Some of the Dartmoor Livestock Preservation Society have now retired, the new contact numbers for animals in distress are, (01364) 73121, (01752) 260067, (01822) 810303 and (01364) 643411.

Some of the many veterinary surgeons that can be contacted are:

Westmoor Veterinary Centre, Tavistock	Tel: (01822) 612561
N. Bowden, Yelverton	Tel: (01822) 854255
J. Edwards, Ivybridge	Tel: (01752) 892700
Okeford Veterinary Centre, Okehampton	Tel: (01837) 52148
Piggot and Arnold, Moretonhampstead	Tel: (01647) 40441
Piggot and Arnold, Bovey Tracey	Tel: (01626) 833023
Rumford, Bond and Baldwin	Tel: (01626) 54260

During July 1995, a child was injured while letterboxing. Not the usual twisted ankle or sprained knee, but caught by the shrapnel of an old World War II shell that exploded when her brother threw it down. Luckily accidents like this are very rare, the army does try to clear up behind it, but if you or your family find a suspicious looking object, DON'T pick it up, but make a note of where it is, and report it to the police, or Dartmoor Ranger when you get off the moor.

Finally, don't forget the Letterboxer's Code and the Country Code, and enjoy your letterboxing. But if you get completely hooked on it . . . don't blame me!